HERNÁN CORTÉS

Conquistador, Colonizer, and Destroyer of the Aztec Empire

JOE GREEK

ROSEN
PUBLISHING®
New York

Published in 2017 by The Rosen Publishing Group, Inc.
29 East 21st Street, New York, NY 10010

Library of Congress Cataloging-in-Publication Data

Names: Greek, Joe, author.
Title: Hernán Cortés : conquistador, colonizer, and destroyer of the Aztec Empire / Joe Greek.
Description: First edition. | New York : Rosen Publishing, 2017. | Series: Spotlight on explorers and colonization | Includes bibliographical references and index. | Audience: Grade 7 to 12.
Identifiers: LCCN 2015050844| ISBN 9781477788127 (library bound) | ISBN 9781477788103 (pbk.) | ISBN 9781477788110 (6-pack)
Subjects: LCSH: Cortés, Hernán, 1485–1547. | Mexico—History—Conquest, 1519–1540. | Mexico—Discovery and exploration—Spanish. | Explorers—Mexico—Biography. | Explorers—Spain—Biography. | Conquerors—Mexico—Biography.
Classification: LCC F1230.C385 G74 2016 | DDC 972.02092—dc23
LC record available at http://lccn.loc.gov/2015050844

Manufactured in the United States of America

CONTENTS

EARLY LIFE IN SPAIN

In 1519, the conquistador Hernán Cortés led an expedition of six hundred men into what is today central Mexico. Considered ruthless by some and brave by others, the Spanish explorer's presence in the New World would create fierce rivalries and bring about the sudden downfall of one of North America's greatest empires—the Aztecs. In the end, his expedition into the unknown would expand the Spanish Empire and ensure that his name would not be forgotten.

Hernán Cortés was born around 1485 in the village of Medellín, Spain. His family came from the lesser nobility. At the age of fourteen, he was sent to the University of Salamanca to study law. With stories of

exploration and adventure spreading throughout Spain, including recent discoveries made by Christopher Columbus in the New World, Cortés soon found a new calling in life. Only two years into school, he dropped out and began making plans to travel to the lands we now know as the Americas.

SETTING SAIL FOR THE NEW WORLD

Only nineteen years old, Cortés set sail in 1504 to the Caribbean island of Hispaniola (which is today Haiti and the Dominican Republic). The journey would have been long and dangerous. Depending on the weather and skill of the ship's captain, the trip could last an entire month or more. Unlike today's ships, which are equipped with modern technology and equipment, the vessels of Cortés's time would often become lost at sea or fall victim to hurricanes or other dangerous storms.

When Cortés safely landed in Santo Domingo, the capital of Hispaniola, he quickly began to establish himself within

Sixteenth-century explorers traveled the seas on large ships, such as this Spanish carrack, that relied on wind power.

the community. The island's governor, Nicolás de Ovando, soon gave him a respectable position within the local government as a notary.

During this time, he also came under the good graces of Diego Velázquez de Cuéllar, an aid to Ovando. The relationship between the two would last several years before ending in betrayal.

CONQUEST OF CUBA

In 1511, Diego Columbus, the oldest son of Christopher Columbus and the newly appointed governor of Hispaniola, selected Velázquez to lead an expedition to the island of Cuba. With four vessels and three hundred soldiers set to sail from the port of Santo Domingo, Velázquez recruited Cortés to join his party.

Once in Cuba, the conquistadors faced little resistance from the island's native inhabitants. Soon, Velázquez and the other Spanish explorers settled the island and formed towns, including Trinidad, Santo Espíritu, Puerto Príncipe, and Santiago de Cuba.

It is said that Cortés was a well-spoken and intelligent individual. His outgoing personality and thirst for exploration helped him rise in the Spanish ranks of power.

Having earned Velázquez's trust, Cortés was given the position of clerk to the treasurer within his government. In this highly respected role, Cortés was responsible for making sure that the Spanish crown received its portion of the riches that were taken from the island. Over time, Cortés secured even more important jobs within Velázquez's government. He was quickly gaining the respect of a growing number of people within the colony.

FIRST STEPS TOWARD MEXICO

By 1517, Cortés's administrative abilities had proved to many settlers in Cuba that he was a natural-born leader. That same year, fellow conquistador Francisco Hernández de Córdoba mistakenly discovered Mexico's Yucatán Peninsula when strong winds sent his ships off course.

Hearing of gold and riches to be found in Mexico, Velázquez sent Juan de Grijalva to explore the mainland in 1518. When word of the rumors was confirmed, the governor ordered Cortés to prepare an expedition to conquer and colonize Mexico.

However, the relationship between Cortés and Velázquez had become strained. Due to family conflicts and jealousy over the growing

Perhaps one of Velázquez's (*second from right*) biggest regrets in his career was his decision to entrust Cortés (*right*) with command of the expedition to Mexico.

popularity of Cortés among Cuba's Spanish inhabitants, the governor came to distrust the conquistador.

Just before Cortés and a force of about six hundred soldiers and sailors were to set sail, the governor called the expedition off. After finding out that Cortés had defiantly embarked on the journey anyway on February 18, 1519, Velázquez charged him with mutiny against the Spanish crown.

MEETING MEXICO'S NATIVES

Cortés and his Spanish fleet spotted the Yucatán coast of Mexico in March 1519. Claiming the land for the Spanish crown, he landed in what is now the state of Tabasco.

Upon their arrival, the Spaniards were met with resistance from the local natives. However, their arrows, rocks, and spears were no match against the cannons and guns of the conquistadors. Perhaps most frightening to the native people, though, was the sight of the Spaniards on horseback. The natives had never seen horses before, and they believed that the rider and horse were actually one.

Quick to make peace, the Tabascans presented Cortés with tributes. Among their gifts were twenty women, including a young woman who would become known as La Malinche. She was also known as Malintzin, as well as by the Spanish name Doña Marina. She would end up serving as an interpreter with the Aztecs. A relationship developed between Cortés and La Malinche, and they would eventually have a son together.

A MESSAGE FROM THE AZTEC RULER

As word of the Spaniards' forceful arrival in Mexico began to spread among the native tribes, the conquistadors sailed further along the coast. On April 20, 1519, the Totonac Indians on the Isle of Sacrifices warmly welcomed Cortés and his fleet. The Totonacs hoped that the Spanish would become their allies and free them from Aztec rule and aggression. The Aztec Empire, ruled by Moctezuma II, forced the smaller nations to pay tributes of gold and other riches.

A few days later, messengers sent by Moctezuma arrived. Climbing aboard

Moctezuma II was viewed as a god by many inhabitants of the Aztec Empire. His ornate armor, jewelry, and colorful clothing only helped to promote this belief.

Cortés's ship, the messengers kissed the ground before him. Then they presented him with gifts of gold, turquoise, armor, and ornate clothing.

To these gestures, Cortés replied, "Is this all?" Then he had them tied up and forced them to watch a demonstration of the Spanish cannons. The power and thundering sound of the cannons caused the Aztecs to faint. Following the display of Spanish might, Cortés sent the messengers back to Moctezuma in the Aztec capital of Tenochtitlán.

MARCHING TOWARD THE AZTEC CAPITAL

When the messengers told Moctezuma of their frightening encounter with Cortés, the great ruler was struck with fear. In his mind, the conquistador represented the possible return of Quetzalcoatl, "the feathered serpent." In Aztec mythology, Quetzalcoatl was an exiled deity who had vowed to reclaim his kingdom.

Meanwhile, Cortés was faced with a dilemma. He could return to Cuba and face the wrath of Velázquez, or he could make his way toward Tenochtitlán. In order to cut his ties with Velázquez, he established a colony that he named Villa Rica de Vera and

Cruz declared himself its captain general.

After learning that some of his men had conspired to steal a ship and return to Cuba, Cortés had the entire fleet scuttled. With no way out, he began a 200-mile (325-kilometer) march toward Tenochtitlán.

Realizing that he could turn the smaller tribes against Moctezuma and the Aztecs, Cortés made alliances with natives as he traveled inland. In many cases, the tribes welcomed the chance to help the Spanish. Some natives, however, were reluctant to join them.

TLAXCALA AND CHOLULA

Upon reaching the territory of the Tlaxcalans, the conquistadors were met with resistance. The Spanish were outnumbered but had horses and more powerful weapons. After several days of fierce fighting, the Tlaxcalans decided to make peace with the Spanish. The Tlaxcalans and the Aztecs were enemies, and they had been fighting a long series of wars against each other. Tlaxcalan leaders decided to ally themselves with the Spanish in the hope of bringing down the Aztec Empire.

From Tlaxcala, the Spanish and their allies continued on toward the city of Cholula. Rumor spread that the Cholulans were planning an ambush. However, when the

The conquistadors are sometimes viewed as heroic explorers. Yet they also carried out massacres, such as the one in Cholula.

Spanish and Tlaxcalans arrived, they found the Cholulan leaders and warriors peacefully gathered at the Temple of Quetzalcoatl. Though unarmed, the Cholulans were surrounded and killed.

The killings in Cholula would be another turning point in the conquest for Cortés. When other tribes heard of the massacre, they learned quickly to submit to the Spaniards. Eventually, Cortés would amass around two hundred thousand native allies before reaching Tenochtitlán.

WELCOMED BY MOCTEZUMA

Cortés, his men, and one thousand Tlaxcalan soldiers arrived at the great city of Tenochtitlán on November 8, 1519. The Aztec capital was located on an island in the shallow Lake Texcoco, giving it the appearance of a floating city. With its massive temples and towers, Cortés referred to it as "the City of Dreams."

As they marched across the land bridges, or causeways, crowds of curious onlookers surrounded the Spaniards. When Cortés finally reached the entrance to the heart of the city, Moctezuma was already waiting.

Placing a necklace of gold and jewels around the conquistador's neck, Moctezuma welcomed Cortés and his men as royal

Tenochtitlan.

guests. The Aztecs showered the visitors with gifts and food and placed them in luxurious apartments.

Even though they had welcomed the conquistadors with open arms, the Aztecs knew Cortés could be ruthless. A fear of what might happen next spread throughout the city as the Spaniards made themselves at home.

CORTÉS TAKES CONTROL

Inside Tenochtitlán, Cortés and the conquistadors were amazed by the architecture and treasures found within the city. They took large amounts of gold and other treasures as they pleased.

At the same time, Cortés knew that he was greatly outnumbered by the Aztecs. Afraid that Moctezuma could plot against him, he had the ruler placed under arrest on November 16. Cortés attempted to rule the city through Moctezuma. However, the Aztecs were losing faith in their leader.

When the city's inhabitants began to show signs of resistance, Cortés held a formal ceremony. In front of his own people,

Most of the buildings of Tenochtitlán, including the Templo Mayor (*left*), were destroyed after the Spanish conquest.

Moctezuma was forced to swear allegiance to the king of Spain.

Additionally, Cortés had Christian images placed on the great pyramid and began to destroy the religious symbols of the Aztecs. The destruction of the Aztec's religious symbols emphasized to the natives that Moctezuma was powerless to protect them.

AN ARREST PARTY COMES FOR CORTÉS

In the following months, Cortés managed to keep the inhabitants of Tenochtitlán under control. Unfortunately, the governor of Cuba had not forgotten the betrayal and embarrassment that Cortés had caused him.

By mid-1520, Cortés learned that Velázquez had sent an arrest party to capture him. Leaving behind eighty conquistadors and several hundred Tlaxcalans under the command of Pedro de Alvarado, Cortés headed back toward the coastal town of Zempoala.

Led by Pánfilo de Narváez, the arrest party consisted of 1,400 Spanish troops. When Cortés reached the coast, he carried

CORTES *acomete de noche el Quartel de Panfilo de Narvaez le...*

out a surprise attack in the middle of the night. The attack was a success, and Narváez surrendered to Cortés.

It was a stroke of luck for Cortés that Velázquez's plan backfired. Instead of bringing down his foe, Velázquez effectively provided him with reinforcements. Narváez's men overwhelmingly sided with Cortés and joined the conquistador on his return to Tenochtitlán.

AZTEC ANGER BOILS OVER

While Cortés was away from Tenochtitlán, Alvarado was left in charge. According to accounts from the Spanish, Alvarado allowed the Aztecs to celebrate the spring festival honoring the god Huitzilopochtli in June 1520. When the Aztecs attempted to sacrifice people, a custom of their religion, Alvarado intervened with deadly force.

Hundreds of Aztecs and their leaders were massacred in the yard of one of the temples. According to the Aztecs, the Spanish killed these people because they wanted to take gold and jewelry from them. One thing is known for sure, and that is

that the Aztec people had neared a breaking point.

When Cortés returned days later, he forced Moctezuma to try to calm his people. The emperor, however, was pelted with stones and arrows. Soon after, Moctezuma died. It is unknown if he died of wounds from the attack or if the Spanish killed him. Once news of his death spread, Cortés had to make a decision.

ESCAPE FROM TENOCHTITLÁN

With Moctezuma dead, Cortés had lost his ability to maintain peace with the Aztec people. Further complicating matters, the Spaniards had become trapped within Tenochtitlán. The Aztecs had destroyed many of the causeways leading out of the city. Food was also becoming scarce.

Vastly outnumbered, Cortés knew that his men and Tlaxcalan allies had to make an escape. In order to cross the broken causeways, Cortés ordered his men to construct a wooden bridge that could be carried through the city.

During the night of June 30, 1520, the conquistadors made their way through the Aztec capital. The city was in an uprising.

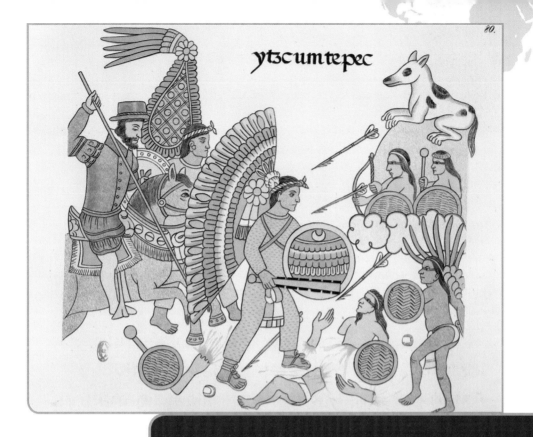

ytzcumtepec

Vastly outnumbered, the conquistadors' escape from the Aztec capital must have been very chaotic.

Thousands of Aztecs attacked the Spanish from canoes and housetops as they fled. Weighed down by the gold they carried, many conquistadors fell into the canals. By the time the Spanish had escaped to relative safety outside of the mountains surrounding Tenochtitlán, hundreds of conquistadors, their horses, and thousands of Tlaxcalan allies were dead.

CORTÉS REGROUPS AS AZTECS FALL ILL

Returning to Tlaxcala, Cortés set out to rebuild his military force. He believed that the defeat of Tenochtitlán was necessary to conquer the Aztecs. Recruiting more Tlaxcalan warriors, Cortés devised a plan to lay siege against the Aztecs by using Lake Texcoco against them. He had a fleet of boats constructed, which the Spanish and their allies could use as the Aztecs had used theirs against them.

Meanwhile, the Aztecs were left with the challenge of cleaning up the aftermath of the battle in Tenochtitlán. Moctezuma's cousin, Cuauhtémoc, took control of the empire. However, the Aztecs had become divided

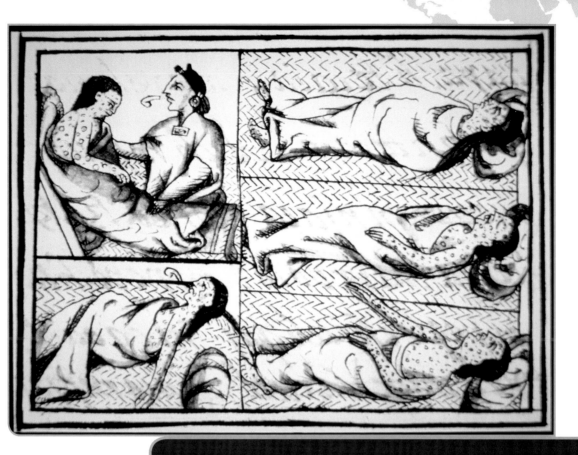

Smallpox devastated the native population of Mexico in the sixteenth century. Its symptoms include painful sores.

and were soon fighting among themselves.

Making matters worse, another foreign enemy of the Aztecs had made itself at home in Tenochtitlán. By December 1520, the deadly disease smallpox—introduced by the Spaniards—spread throughout the capital. With no idea of how to treat the disease and no immunity to it, many Aztecs died.

THE FALL OF THE AZTEC EMPIRE

At the end of 1520, Cortés and his allied forces began a slow march back toward Tenochtitlán. Along the way, they aligned with neighboring territories or conquered them when they resisted.

Around eight thousand natives carried the boats that Cortés had ordered the construction of over mountains and through jungles. When Cortés reached the southern end of the capital, he fought his way through the city street by street. Slowly, the estimated three hundred thousand Aztec defenders that remained were pushed to the northern part of the city. There, they attempted to hold off the invaders for eighty days.

CONQVISTA DE MEXICO POR CORTES..A.7

When all seemed lost, Cuauhtémoc met with Cortés on August 13, 1521, and conceded defeat. In a demeaning gesture, Cortés patted the Aztec leader on the head. The meeting effectively marked the end of the Aztec Empire and solidified Cortés as one of Spain's greatest explorers and conquers of the New World.

THE CONQUEROR OF NEW SPAIN

Having defeated the Aztec Empire and changed the name of Tenochtitlán to Mexico City, Cortés had established himself as ruler of a vast territory from the Caribbean Sea to the Pacific Ocean. Still, the bad blood between Velázquez and Cortés persisted.

Determined to seek revenge against Cortés, Velázquez launched a political attack on the conquistador in Spain. Enlisting the help of the powerful bishop Juan Rodríguez de Fonseca, Velázquez argued to Charles V that Cortés should be brought to justice for treason against the crown.

In his defense, Cortés wrote five lengthy letters to Charles that outlined his actions and the benefits that he had brought to

Spain. Satisfied that Cortés had acted honorably in the name of the crown, Charles officially appointed him as governor, captain general, and chief justice of New Spain. To prevent Cortés from acting on his own in the future, officials were sent to the New World to provide oversight of the new territory.

FALL FROM POWER

An explorer at heart, Cortés was restless when it came to governing New Spain. In 1524, he led a two-year expedition into the jungles of Honduras. While he was away, the officials left in charge of New Spain seized his property and were reckless in governing.

Concerned by news from New Spain, the Spanish government sent a commission, including the judge Luis Ponce de León, to investigate. When Ponce de León died soon after his arrival, Cortés was accused of poisoning him. The accusation forced Cortés into retirement.

In 1528, Cortés returned to Spain to plead with the king to be reinstated as the governor of New Spain. Charles gave him

the noble title marqués del Valle but did not give him his old position back. After a few years, Cortés returned to New Spain and retreated to his estate south of Mexico City, where he built a palace. He also became involved in the exploration of the Pacific Coast.

FINAL EXPEDITION AND DEATH

Cortés returned to Spain in 1540 an embittered man. For years, his reputation had been the subject of attack from his rivals. Rumors that he had murdered his first wife, Catalina Xuárez, in 1522 had even resurfaced.

Refusing to let his name and legacy be smeared further, he convinced Charles V to let him take part in an expedition against the Ottoman Empire in 1541. Charles himself led the attack on Algiers, in what is now Algeria. The expedition, however, was unsuccessful. Cortés died in 1547 near the city of Seville from a lung illness.

This map shows the siege of Algiers in 1541. Cortés was among the Spaniards who took part in the attack.

Cortés's body was moved to New Spain in 1566. There, his remains moved between locations several times. Following the independence of Mexico from Spain in 1821, his remains were hidden within the Hospital of Jesus for more than 120 years. When they were rediscovered in 1946, he was finally laid to rest in the Church of the Immaculate Conception and Jesus the Nazarene in Mexico City.

A DISPUTED LEGACY

From what is known of the life of Hernán Cortés, history has painted two pictures. The first is one of a courageous explorer, a seeker of adventure, and a natural-born leader.

On the other hand, history cannot deny the fact that Cortés was often ruthless and deceptive in the way he dealt with others. The massacre of unarmed natives at the Temple of Quetzalcoatl in Cholula demonstrated his willingness to use violence when it wasn't absolutely necessary. Secondly, his decision to ignore the orders of Velázquez in 1519 showed that he was willing to betray others if it helped him to succeed personally.

Depending on whom you ask, Cortés was either a hero or a villain. Still, his impact on the world cannot be underestimated.

While it is easy to paint the explorer in one light or another, his impact during the discovery of the New World cannot be underestimated. The fall of the Aztecs and the subsequent spread of Christianity by the Spanish helped lead to the formation of modern-day Mexico.

GLOSSARY

allies People, groups, or countries that work together for mutual benefit.

canals Waterways, similar to rivers but built by people, allowing boats to travel inland.

colony An area that is under the control of a foreign country and inhabited by people from that country.

conquistador Explorers from Spain who conquered parts of the Americas in the sixteenth century.

expedition A journey taken by a group with the aim of exploration, research, or war.

fleet A group of ships sailing together and led by one commander.

immunity The human body's ability to resist foreign organisms that can cause disease.

massacre The act of killing a large group of people on purpose with the use of substantial violence.

mutiny To defy the orders of an authority.

mythology A collection of stories that belong to a specific culture.

notary An individual who performs certain legal duties, such as writing contracts or deeds.

port A town or city along a river or sea coast where ships load and unload cargo or passengers.

scuttled Sank a ship on purpose by allowing water to flow into its hull.

tributes Things given to an individual, group, or authority as a sign of respect or dependence.

Field Museum
1400 South Lake Shore Drive
Chicago, IL 60605
(312) 922-9410
Website: http://www.fieldmuseum.org
The Field Museum is one of the largest natural history
   museums in the world. It contains collections of
   artwork and artifacts from around the world that
   tell the story of human beings. The museum hosts
   a large collection of Aztec pottery and artifacts.

Gilder Lehrman Institute of American History
49 West 45th Street, 6th Floor
New York, NY 10036
(646) 366-9666
Website: http://www.gilderlehrmen.org
This nonprofit organization is dedicated to improving
   history education through programs for schools,
   teachers, and students. The groups website also
   provides access to more than sixty thousand
   historical documents.

Mariner's Museum and Park
100 Museum Drive
Newport News, VA 23606
(757) 596-2222
Website: http://www.marinersmuseum.org

One of the largest maritime museums in North America, the Mariner's Museum and Park provides visitors with an overview of the history of human beings and the sea. The museum contains thousands of artifacts and artwork, including items from the Spanish conquest of the New World.

Mexican Museum
2 Marina Boulevard, Building D
San Francisco, CA 94123
(415) 202-9700
Website: http://www.mexicanmuseum.org
Since 1975, The Mexican Museum has promoted the arts and culture of Mexico through exhibits and programs. The museum contains a large collection of historical pieces and artwork, which includes artifacts from the era of Spanish colonization.

Websites

Because of the changing nature of Internet links, Rosen Publishing has developed an online list of websites related to the subject of this book. This site is updated regularly. Please use this link to access the list:

http://www.rosenlinks.com/SEC/cortes

Abnett, Dan. *Hernan Cortes and the Fall of the Aztec Empire* (Jr. Graphic Biographies). New York, NY: Rosen Classroom, 2006.

Apte, Sunita. *The Aztec Empire* (True Books: Ancient Civilizations). New York, NY: Scholastic Corporation, 2010.

Green, Jen. *Aztecs* (Flashback History). New York, NY: Rosen Publishing, 2010.

Gunderson, Jessica. *Conquistadors* (Fearsome Fighters). Mankato, MN: The Creative Company, 2012.

Macdonald, Fiona. *The Aztec and Mayan Worlds* (Passport to the Past). New York, NY: Rosen Publishing, 2009.

Maestro, Betsy, and Giulio Maestro. *Exploration and Conquest: The Americas After Columbus: 1500–1620* (American Story). New York, NY: HarperCollins, 1997.

Mathews, Sally Schofer. *The Sad Night: The Story of an Aztec Victory and a Spanish Loss*. New York, NY: Houghton Mifflin Harcourt, 2001.

Stein, R. Conrad. *The Conquistadores: Building a Spanish Empire in the Americas* (Proud Heritage: the Hispanic Library). North Mankato, MN: The Child's World, 2004.

BIBLIOGRAPHY

Cortés, Hernán. "Cortés on La Noche Triste or the
Night of Sorrows." American Historical Association.
Retrieved December 6, 2015 (https://www
.historians.org).

Federer, Bill. "The Violent Conquest of Mexico." WND
TV, December 1, 2015 (http://www.wnd.com).

Garsd, Jasmine. "Despite Similarities, Pocahontas
Gets Love, Malinche Gets Hate. Why?" NPR,
November 25, 2015 (http://www.npr.org).

Hernandez, Duque Hernández. "The Ever-Moving
Tomb of Hernán Cortés." Mexico News Network,
July 10, 2015 (http://www.mexiconewsnetwork.com).

Jones, Jonathan. "A Brief History of the Aztec
Empire." *Guardian*, September 16, 2009 (http://
www.theguardian.com).

Kukaswadia, Atif. "What Killed The Aztecs?
A Researcher Probes Role of 16th Century
Megadrought." The Public Library of Science, July
30, 2013 (http://blogs.plos.org/).

Levy, Buddy. *Conquistador: Hernán Cortés, King
Montezuma, and the Last Stand of the Aztecs*. New
York, NY: Bantam Books, 2008.

Staff. "On the Trail of Hernán Cortés." *Economist*,
December 20, 2014 (http://www.economist.com).

Wood, Michael. "The Story of the Conquistadors."
BBC, March 29, 2011 (http://www.bbc.co.uk).

INDEX

About the Author

Joe Greek is a writer living in Middle Tennessee. He has written books for middle school students on a variety of historical topics, including the Holocaust and World War I. He lived in Mexico for a period of time and researched the native tribes that had once inhabited the modern-day state of Jalisco.

Photo Credits